Barn Owls

Nocturnal Hunters

Rebecca Rissman

Heinemann
LIBRARY

Chicago, Illinois

Edited by Brynn Baker, Clare Lewis, and Helen Cox Cannons
Designed by Kyle Grenz and Tim Bond
Picture research by Tracy Cummins
Production by Helen McCreath
Originated by Capstone Global Library Ltd
Printed and bound in China by Leo Paper Group

18 17 16 15 14
10 9 8 7 6 5 4 3 2 1

Library of Congress Cataloging-in-Publication Data

ISBN 978-1-4846-0310-9 (hardcover)
ISBN 978-1-4846-0316-1 (paperback)
ISBN 978-1-4846-0328-4 (ebook PDF)

Acknowledgments
We would like to thank the following for permission
to reproduce photographs:FLPA: Derek Middleton, 7
mouse, Erica Olsen, 19, Gary K Smith, 21, Imagebroker,
5, 23d, Michael Durham/Minden Pictures, 7 bat, Paul
Sawer, 17, Simon Litten, 20, 23c; Getty Images: Derrick
Hamrick, 1, 23g, Oxford Scientific/Michael Leach, front
cover; Science Source: Kenneth M. Highfill, 9; Shutter-
stock: Andrew Astbury, 7 fox, CreativeNature.nl, 10, Dr.
Morley Read, 14, 15, 23e, Gerckens-Photo-Hamburg, 18,
23f, iceeyes198369, 6, Mark Bridger, 4, 23a, back cover,
Miles Away Photography, 22, Stephen Mcsweeny, 12,
Tom Reichner, 11, Piotr Krzeslak, 7 hedgehog;
Superstock: imagebroker.net, 16, 23b

Every effort has been made to contact copyright holders
of material reproduced in this book. Any omissions will
be rectified in subsequent printings if notice is given to
the publisher.

All the Internet addresses (URLs) given in this book
were valid at the time of going to press. However, due to
the dynamic nature of the Internet, some addresses may
have changed, or sites may have changed or ceased to
exist since publication. While the author and publisher
regret any inconvenience this may cause readers, no
responsibility for any such changes can be accepted by
either the author or the publisher.

Contents

What Is a Barn Owl?. 4

What Does Nocturnal Mean? 6

Where Do Barn Owls Live? 8

What Do Barn Owls Eat? 10

How Do Barn Owls Find Prey? 12

What Are Owl Pellets?. 14

What Are Baby Barn Owls Like? 16

Do Barn Owls Have Predators? 18

How Can You Spot Barn Owls? 20

Barn Owl Body Map. 22

Picture Glossary 23

Find Out More. 24

Index 24

What Is a Barn Owl?

A barn owl is a large bird. Its body is covered in gray or brown feathers.

It has light-colored feathers on its face.

A barn owl has sharp claws called talons. It has large eyes and a strong **beak**.

You rarely see barn owls during the day because they are **nocturnal**.

What Does Nocturnal Mean?

Animals that are nocturnal are awake at night.

Nocturnal animals sleep during the day.

bat

fox

hedgehog

mouse

Many animals are nocturnal.

Bats, foxes, hedgehogs, and mice are nocturnal.

Where Do Barn Owls Live?

Barn owls live in Europe, North America, South America, Africa, Asia, and Australia.

They can live in forests, fields, deserts, farmlands, and even in cities.

Barn owls make nests in trees, caves, and buildings.

They are called barn owls because they often make nests in barns.

What Do Barn Owls Eat?

Barn owls hunt for nocturnal animals.

They usually eat small animals, such as mice and bats.

Some barn owls even eat larger animals, such as baby rabbits.

Barn owls also eat other small birds.

How Do Barn Owls Find Prey?

Barn owls have very good hearing. They listen for **prey**.

Barn owls also have good eyesight. They can see small animals moving in the dark.

Barn owls fly quietly after prey.
They catch prey with their sharp talons.

What Are Owl Pellets?

Owls often swallow their prey whole.

After they eat, they spit out **pellets**.

Pellets are the bones, fur, and feathers of owl prey.

Pellets show the different animals an owl has eaten.

What Are Baby Barn Owls Like?

Female barn owls lay eggs in springtime.

Owl chicks are covered in **down** shortly after they hatch.

The mother owl brings prey back to the nest to feed the chicks.

Young owls leave the nest after two months.

Do Barn Owls Have Predators?

Barn owls have few **predators**.

In some places, raccoons, cats, and larger owls eat barn owl chicks.

Humans can harm barn owls too.

Growing cities and new buildings can make it hard for barn owls to find enough prey to eat.

How Can You Spot Barn Owls?

Barn owls are easiest to spot at **dusk**. Watch for them swooping low over fields.

Owl droppings and pellets can tell you that a nest is nearby.

Listen for barn owl screeches. They can sometimes tell you where a nest is.

Barn Owl Body Map

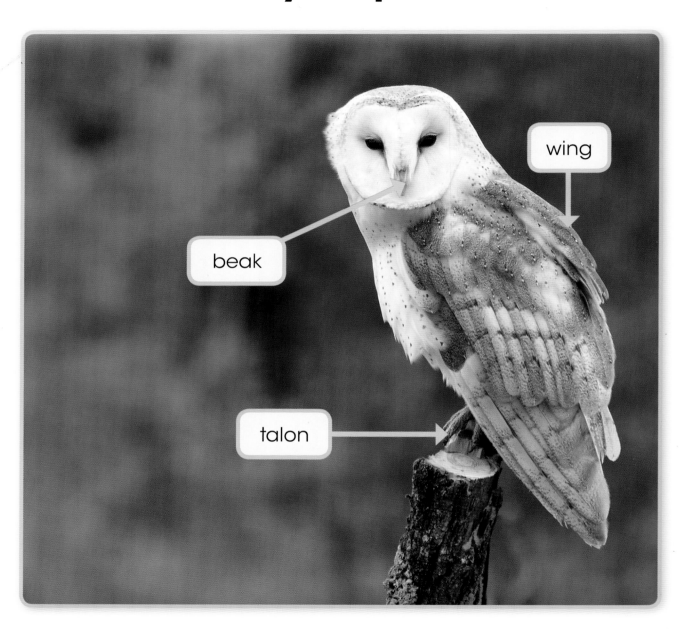

wing

beak

talon

Picture Glossary

 beak a bird's hard jaw

 down soft, fluffy feathers of a young bird

 dusk time of day when the sun sets

 nocturnal awake at night and asleep during the day

 pellet bones, fur, and feathers of owl prey

 predator animal that hunts other animals for food

 prey animal that is hunted by other animals

Find Out More

Books

Bodden, Valerie. *Owls.* Amazing Animals. Mankato, Minn.: Creative Education, 2013.

Dunn, Mary R. *Owls.* Nocturnal Animals. Mankato, Minn.: Capstone Press, 2012.

Websites

Discover more about barn owls at:
http://allaboutbirds.org/guide/Barn_Owl/id

Learn more about owls at:
http://bbc.co.uk/nature/life/owl

Index

barns 9
beaks 5, 22
bones 15
buildings 9, 19
cats 18
caves 9
chicks 16, 17, 18
cities 8, 19
claws 5

deserts 8
down 16
droppings 21
dusk 20
eggs 16
eyes 5, 12
farmlands 8
feathers 4, 15
fields 20

food 10, 11
fur 15
grasslands 8
humans 19
nests 9, 17, 21
pellets 14, 15, 21
predators 18
prey 12, 13, 14, 15,
   17, 19

rabbits 11
raccoons 18
spring 16
talons 5, 13, 22
trees 9
wings 22
woodlands 8